D1632026

About the author

Lucy is a London-based creator by day, an illustrator by night, and a singer-songwriter by accident. Her back catalogue of hits includes 'Don't Send Girls Pictures of Your Penis' and 'The Dating App Rap' to name a few ...

She has combined her love of observational comedy and doodling on her Instagram page @thedoodlemaestro.

Swipe Left is her first book.

HQ

An imprint of HarperCollinsPublishers Ltd.

1 London Bridge Street

London SE1 9GF

This paperback edition 2019

1

First published in Great Britain by HQ, an imprint of HarperCollinsPublishers Ltd. 2019

Copyright © Lucy Baker 2019

Lucy Baker asserts the moral right to be identified as the author of this work

A catalogue record for this book is available from the British Library

ISBN: 978-0-00-833445-1

Printed and bound in Slovenia by GPS Group

Design by Steve Wells

CONTENTS

Dear Reader,

A little while ago, I was in the darkest depths of singledom. I hadn't dated anyone in a long time, it was utter desperation-stations. So, I did what any normal twenty-something would do … I downloaded dating apps and started swiping furiously. Determined to find the man of my dreams.

The reality was disappointing.

Though there were a select few profiles with potential, far too many fell into the 'swipe left' category. From bathroom selfies to clunky bios, and some seriously questionable chat-up lines, the outlook seemed bleak.

But all was not lost.

Instead of despairing over Mike 29's loo-mirror grimace, I decided to take action. I started noting down the things that I thought were appealing in a profile, and the things that would send anyone running for the hills. Friends offered up their own hilariously awkward anecdotes. And so, *Swipe Left* came to be.

I hope you find it useful, or at the very least amusing. But more than anything, I hope it gets you a truly great date.

Lucy

CHAPTER 1. PROFILE DON'TS

Don't have a million people in your picture. This isn't a game of Where's Wally.

Wally, 22

I'm the bloke waving.

Don't be a catfish. They're going to find out what you look like eventually.

Don't hide your face. You might end up dating someone IRL (hurray). In which case they'll need to know what you actually look like.

Don't use your LinkedIn photo. You ain't gonna get endorsed on here honey.

Sharon, 22
Skilled in Excel, Microsoft Word & Adobe.
Endorsed for teamwork, management, accounting and
photocopying.

Don't use selfies.
There are only two conclusions to the selfie:

1. You don't have friends
2. You are intolerably vain

But if you really insist, for heaven's sake
DON'T DO IT IN THE BATHROOM.

Sasha, 27
Even fitter in real life dw (if that's even possible hahahah).
#seflie #me #inthebathroom
#didImentionIamincrediblyattractive

KEEP CALM
AND
CARRY ON
BEING
INCREDIBLY
GOOD LOOKING

Jason, 35
Looking for a girl who thinks I'm as amazing as I think I am. You can usually find me in the bathroom, tensing my worldy biceps.

Don't post pictures where you're romantically engaged with somebody else. You're sending out the wrong message.

Mark, 31

DW, she's my sister.

Don't lie about your age ...

Don't have a photo with someone much better looking than you … you're just setting yourself up for failure.

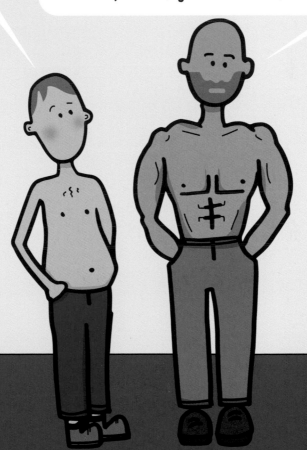

CHAPTER 2. PROFILE DO'S

Demonstrate your passions, whatever they may be!

Show some variety with each photo.
Be creative. Express yourself!

Mo, 28
Life's no struggle when ya know how to juggle.

For goodness sake, SMILE!

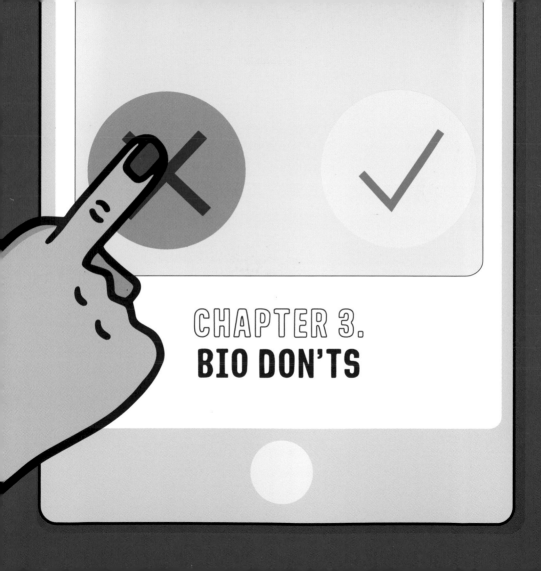

CHAPTER 3.
BIO DON'TS

DON'T POST EVERYTHING IN
CAPITAL LETTERS. PEOPLE WILL THINK YOU
ARE A BIT OF A NUTTER.

Same goes for exclamation marks!!!!!!!!!
Resist using more than two at a time!!!!!!!!!!!
Exclamation marks are like cats.
Any more than two and it makes
you look weird.

Rob, 31

Lover of cats, custard creams and Poirot!!!!!!!!!!! Very easy going !!!!!!!!! Swipe right!!!!!!!!! Been single for quite a long time but very happy with it haha!!!!!

Don't talk about your preference
for a weight, people will just think you're a
complete dick. Because you are.

Don't lie about what you like doing. You might find yourself in a real pickle.

Don't say your favourite person / dream dinner guest is David Attenborough. Everyone's favourite person is David Attenborough, and frankly we're bored of it. Louis Theroux for that matter too.

Don't be too prescriptive in who
you're looking for ...

Josh, 31

I'm looking for a 29-year-old, 5 foot 7, brunette model. Must own a home with decent acreage and a sports car. Must have a golden Labrador, purebred. Must know at least one person called Tarquin. Descendant of the royal family preferable but not entirely necessary if other attributes have been met.

She. Does. Not. Exist.

Don't pretend you're 6 foot 7 when you're 5 foot 1. They'll find out. Tell the truth. The chances are, they'll like you anyway!

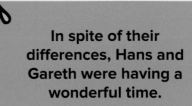
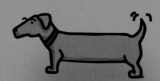

Don't go overkill on the emojis.
Throw a couple of words in there too.

CHAPTER 4.
BIO DO'S

Show your sense of humour.

Tobi, 26

I guess you could say I'm a fun-ghi.

Be honest about what you're there for.

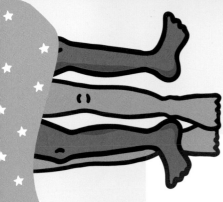

PEACE
BRO

WAAAAAAAAHHHHHHH!!!

I'm looking for ...

... the love of my life
... a cheeky shag
... a girlfriend / boyfriend
... someone who wants
to have kids
... a fellow hippie
... someone to snog occasionally
... my car keys

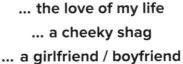

Phoebe, 21
Student by day, bread maker by night! Why? Because I kneed the dough. Looking for a fellow culture-vulture to visit galleries and eat pastries with.

Phoebe, 21
So I'm currently studying at Edinburgh University. Don't get me wrong it's a great university but the course I'm doing is pretty complex and they keep assigning me the wrong bloody modules. How am I meant to get a 2:1 if the entire infrastructure of the uni is a complete shambles?!?!? Anyway. Back to what I was saying. I am an avid baker, currently tackling a 'sourdough starter': basically how you do it is to mix 500g of the flour with the apple and water. Tip this into an airtight container and mark the level on the outside of the container (so you can see whether the mix has risen). Cover and leave to ferment for 3 days. It's easier than it looks, don't worry. Do you like baking? Swipe right if so.

Keep your bio short & snappy.

Look to the future, don't dwell on the past.

Sam, 23
Looking to meet a guy with a GREAT sense of humour, who shares my love of Korean Pop, poodles, pot noodles & sci-fi.

Sam, 23
Still in love with my ex-boyfriend, Steve, who dumped me because I was 'too clingy'. CLINGY?!?!?!? HAH. I'll show you clingy, Steve. I'm on a DATING APP NOW. I'VE MOVED ON. Swipe right if you're interested.

CHAPTER 5.

MESSAGING DON'TS

Don't ghost people. Unless you are a ghost. In which case, ghost away.

Casper, 31
Very friendly.

Don't send pictures of your privates,
ESPECIALLY if they haven't asked
for them ...

1. If you don't know them you can't
   trust they won't show other people

2. It ruins all the mystery

3. It ain't that pretty

Don't give out your personal details
until you've met them.

If the other person decides they don't wish to pursue the conversation further, don't hound, beg or criticise. Respect their decision and move on. You'll look better for doing it.

Don't just reply with YES / NO answers.
They'll soon tire of you!

CHAPTER 6.

MESSAGING DO'S

Once you've matched,
get chatting straight away.

It's a match!
Start the conversation.

December 2017

Heyy Phyllis!
How's it going? U good?

December 2019

Sorry Dan. I'm married
now with a 4-month-old baby.

Ah cool. No worries.

If in doubt, use a pun.

Gareth, 34
Easy-going guy.
I love cheese & wine.
Looking for a girl who shares my passion.

Gareth! Sorry this might sound a little cheesy. But you're the man-chego I've been looking for. Un-brie-lievable profile, I've never seen anyone feta.

Hey Laura, hah thank you!

Don't want to put you under any Cheshire but do you fancy a drink soon?

There's stil(a)ton of things I'd like to know about you.

Be truthful about your own interests.
You're here to meet someone who likes
you for who you are.

Once you've chatted for a while and gained their trust, for goodness sake ask them on a date!

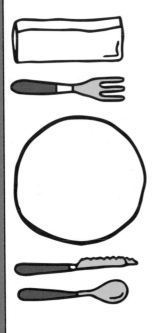

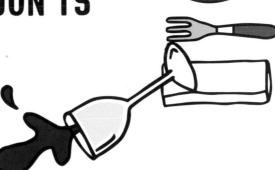

CHAPTER 7.

FIRST
DATE
DON'TS

Don't take them anywhere where they might think you're about to murder them or where they could murder you.
Go somewhere public, just in case.

Bad opening lines.

Don't reveal how much you already know about them. Even though you've done the inevitable Facebook / Instagram / LinkedIn stalk, PLEASE try and pretend you haven't.

Two weeks earlier, Sally conducted some light research ...

Don't order spaghetti. It's carnage.
Or anything garlicky for that matter.

Don't just talk about yourself.

Don't make any grand declarations
of love straight away.

Don't plan your entire lives together before you've got to know them.

PINTEREST BOARD – Mrs Rose Bloom

INVITATION

You are cordially invited to the wedding
of Jackson Bloom & Rosemary
Fannington

They met on a dating app
12.08.2019

St Matthew's Church

DON'T get the same Tube / bus home,
it makes for an awkward goodbye.

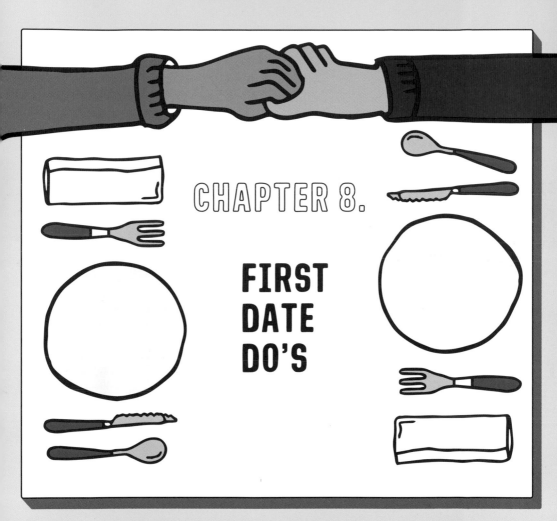

CHAPTER 8.

FIRST
DATE
DO'S

Ask them lots of questions.

Go somewhere where there are things to talk about.

Pick a place where you can
actually hear them.

Go somewhere affordable.

Have an exit strategy.

Playing games can be a fun way to ease the nerves.

Just don't get too competitive …

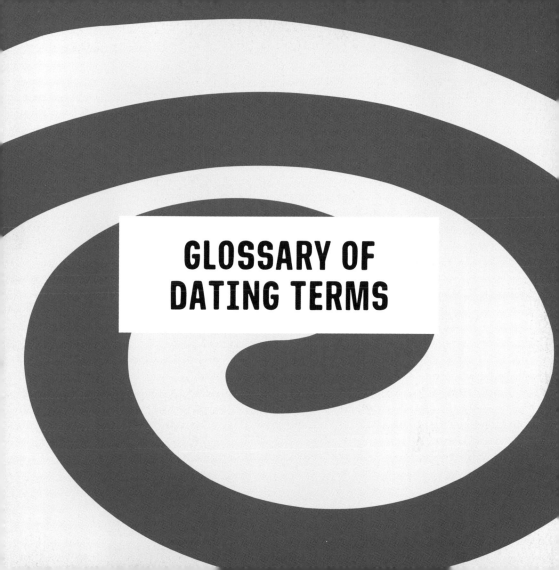

GLOSSARY OF
DATING TERMS

BREADCRUMBING

The act of sending out flirtatious, but non-committal text messages (i.e. 'breadcrumbs') in order to lure a sexual partner without expending much effort.

CUSHIONING

If you're 'cushioning' someone, it means you're dating them but you don't think it's going to end well. Instead of cutting loose, you prepare for the break-up by chatting and flirting with several other people, to cushion the blow when it happens.

GHOSTING

When a person cuts off all communication with the person they're dating, with zero warning or notice beforehand. You'll mostly see them avoiding phone calls, social media and public spaces.

ORBITING

When the person who ghosted you,
continues to linger in your life by watching
every single one of your Instagram
stories and liking / commenting on
your social media posts.

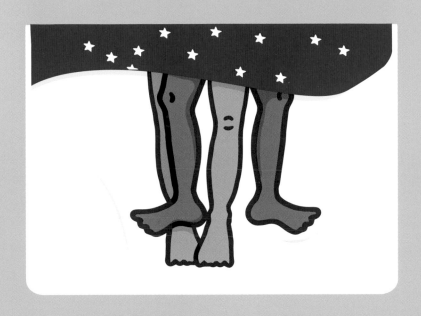

Alternatives:
Amazon Prime & Sexy Time
DVD and D in V
BBC iPlayer & I Play Her
HBO & Fellatio

STASHING

When the person you're dating doesn't introduce you to their friends or family, and doesn't post about you on social media. Basically, you're their secret boyfriend or girlfriend, while they feel justified in 'stashing' you in the corner, pretending nothing is going on to the outside world.

ZOMBIE-ING

Ghosters who decide to resurface are 'zombies'.
Zombie-ing usually occurs a fair amount of time after
they disappeared into thin air. Often acting like nothing
happened like a smug, re-animated corpse.

CATCH AND RELEASE

When someone puts all their effort into flirtatious texts, and trying to date you, until they 'catch' you. Then, when you finally agree to the date, they immediately lose interest.

CATFISHING

The term 'catfish' was coined by the documentary film *Catfish* by Henry Joost and Ariel Schulman, and refers to when a person lures someone into a relationship by pretending to be someone else in an online platform.

KITTENFISHING

'Kittenfishing' is like a less severe form of catfishing. It refers to when you present yourself in an unrealistically positive way on your dating apps — for example, by only using photos that are years out of date or heavily edited, or lying about your age, job, height, and hobbies.

CUFFING

When winter is on its way you grab the nearest person to you and couple up, to save spending those chilly winter nights alone.

Do you love me?

No. I'm just using you for your body heat.

Fair play.

Cheeky mother-cuffer.

MONKEYING

When you move from one relationship to the next without any time in-between, like a monkey swinging from the branches of a tree.

PEACOCKING